D0732193

The
Hayflick
Limit

Matthew
Tierney

Coach House Books | Toronto

first edition

 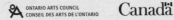

Published with the generous assistance of the Canada Council for the Arts and the Ontario Arts Council. Coach House Books also acknowledges the support of the Government of Ontario through the Ontario Book Publishing Tax Credit and the Government of Canada through the Book Publishing Industry Development Program.

LIBRARY AND ARCHIVES CANADA CATALOGUING IN PUBLICATION

Tierney, Matthew Frederick, 1970-
       The hayflick limit / Matthew Tierney.

ISBN 978-1-55245-217-2

       I. Title.

PS8589.I42H39 2009   C811'.6   C2009-901243-X

For my parents

TABLE OF CONTENTS

GROUND CONTROL

ZUGZWANG

BODY COUNT

THE NEWLY ENDURING

Time equals cold. Each body, sooner
or later, falls prey to a telescope.
– Joseph Brodsky

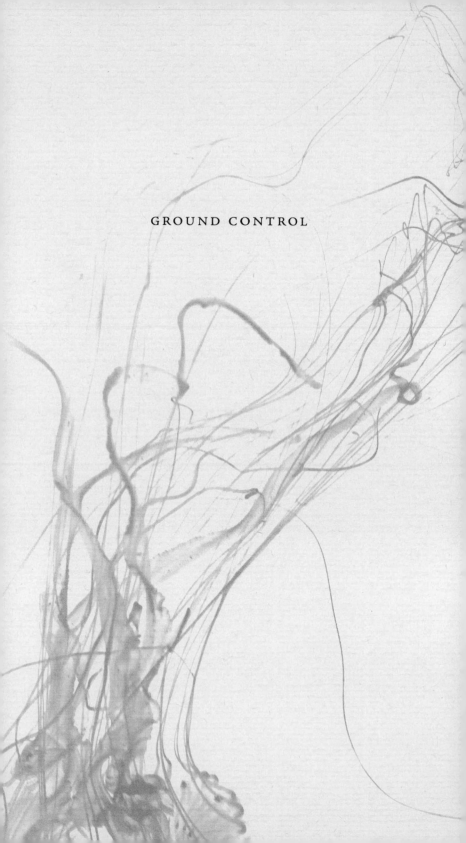

GROUND CONTROL

Each instant, O it mushrooms, so many
        options, a foaming cloud
of nows: more shut-eye, up and head to the can,
            scratch my ear or stand

and spin, counter-clockwise, twice … all
        tentative. Infinite I
diverges in the woods, one laughs, ten more sob,
            piss their pants, succumb

to anomie. In the lineup of faux me's, a single
        McCoy. Hints? Apathy
turns my crank. Blinking is necessary, it moistens
            the cornea. I smile

to mask emotion, carry the gene that allows
        tongue rolling. So weigh
the odds, ride waves of surely-nots and bang-ons,
            map my presents. I'm

a sum over histories, one zillisecond at a time,
        most likely supine, massaging
my temples, eye on that mushroom cloud looming
            in the middle distance. You?

THE ECLIPSE CHASER

Always got a soft spot
for your first: Kenya, 1981,
six minutes of nirvana packed
into my noggin and parcelled out
over the worst of my everyday –
open houses for fixer-uppers,
clients' tears, rubber cheques, snags
in my pantyhose – till Java in '83
restocked my memory with a swath
of E-time, just enough fuel for
a thank-god-no-kids divorce.
Mexico got me off the bottle,
come Romania I was already
agent number one four years
running. I've clocked 26 minutes
all told, in the black, yet
it's the donkey's years in realty
that sweep past in a finger snap.
A little secret, I'm old enough
to be your mother, so listen close –
nothing, nothing will rouse
those rosy little cheeks of yours
quite like a total eclipse.

Do us a favour, dear, poke
the fire. Nice. Takes the fight
to that creak there, behind my knees.

Truer words … nights like these
are a heavy cross. All your lovers
pass in the glaze, the promises
nearly kept, their meaning lost,

13

each face ablaze with longing
for you-know-not-what.
Take my word: noon tomorrow,
when that opal necklace is clasped
over the new moon's nape, you'll
have your question; and when
the chromosphere forges a ring
around that black disc, last light
a cherry diamond brighter than
bright, you'll be all answer.

Near as one can get? Eyes
closed, tight now! On the backs
of your lids, the corona,
a boys' choir in white robes
sustaining a high C. Keep them
shut, it's poetry or nothing, missy,
that char eye in the day sky, pure
gobsmack. I see how you frown,
the doubt in your shoulders, but
there's nothing more to tell.
T minus ten hours till
we glimpse light once forbidden.
That's all, dear. The two of us,
timeless bridesmaids of the sun.

APEIROPHOBIA
fear of infinity

Uncaged. Run from it,
go ahead, try. Wherever you are
it's there. Cousin to zero

with none of the zip, winking
from vanishing points as though
innocent, a party trick. Face it

with no illusions. That sucking sound
is the centre of the universe
voided from its nest

in the mind. Even Aristotle
turned a blind eye, afraid of disproving
God. Shameless modern mortals

and the games they play, spurning bliss
for the oil-slickened hand
of calculus, lifespans spun

into Spirographs, giddy
paths to nowhere. The chill comes
at the never-end of forever, tingle

in your fingers a surefire tell.
Eternity is devil's work, just
look at its mark – double coil of

a serpent eating its tail.
There's no way of unknowing
what we know.

Fernando's waiting for sirens. His 1500 sq. ft. 2 bdrm., 2 baths holds one ergonomic chair, oblique to the window. Storeys below, traffic iterates simple patterns while figures close the gaps, one side of the street to the other. Sometimes he hums. His voice returns to him off oak wood flooring and drywall, knits the space between one siren and the next. After work till 4 a.m., pencil held like a knife, five years of raw data buttering the loose paper around his sock feet. Factor analysis reveals frequency peaks at rush hour, escalates late in the week. Friday nights he throws in another variable for fun. The S&P 500, the line on the basketball game. Once, Yahoo! blew its fourth quarter and sirens tick-tocked long past dinner until the Raptors covered the spread. Like ice cream, that day. Fernando upped the stakes when he added a final column to track his mood. Nine grades of 'good,' nine 'bad.' Sixteen months and a scatter plot later, Fernando's got something all right: correlation coefficient is positively dead-on. The numbers can only mean one thing – he's willing the sirens to life. Fernando feels the hidden power quicken within. Finally! A surge of well-being sends him slip-sliding to the fridge for a tub of Neapolitan. Meanwhile the city burns, a conflagration of red piercing lights.

The soul-searching over first principles. Some
swear by salt, Nature jogging our memory

of wounds; there's water to clean them, or
that earliest syllabic for *Why?*, even more so

the hereditary function of the genome:
Michael Jordan skywalking towards the basket,

the air apparent. Of the four-letter words,
fuck and *love* are the ones we set store by

while God looks on, right of centre, greatly
exaggerated. Take carbon, its limitless ability

to bond, such chains of harmony unsung
by the masses. Radiohead's third album? OK

but Mozart's Requiem is written in the script
and we're still mapping the human brain,

its blips and dark seas, unravellings, the lucid
dream of a life lived. That we only use 10 percent

makes for good copy, bad Einstein.
What creatures! To deny our fullness;

to deconstruct chance happenings: hailstorms,
bull markets, ex-wife on a beach in sunny

Cancun. To presume a final answer
before counting the grains of sand.

PARELASIPHOBIA
fear of parades

As if real life
weren't Byzantine enough.
Under a xenon-charged sky, floats

float by. A high school band sweats out
Sgt. Pepper epaulettes
and worsted slacks, bleating

a half-tempo 'When the Saints
Go Marching In,' while the majorettes
in red-spangled spandex

pause in formation, puffy arms poised,
for batons to fall like
day stars, sons of morning –

a go-kart zips past,
Methuselah in a fez, shepherding
fellow Lions Club members

in their tramp to the end.
A peril of fools. Nonsense
is Munchkinland: only

the unfocused, peripheral eye
catches the curls of green smoke,
the long road lined

with scarecrows.

It stands here still, stands vibrant as you pass,
The invisible, untoppled omphalos.
— Seamus Heaney

No more innocently taking down a building.
Between major avenues, off a side street, what's left
fenced in to protect the pedestrian, demolition cranes
unmanned, watchful. Bank towers glide over
the uglified stub, floors one through four shorn
of their non-load-bearing. A clench, standing.
Square to the December sky, a line graph descending.
Electrical cables and rebar become installation in the flail
and fall from structure; cross-sectioned walls pullulate
with the unplugged, suspend concrete chunks in a metal nest
while the rest, flensed, flayed, gnawed at by wind,
airbrushes the crown with egg-white dust.
A new millennium ganglion, thrust.
Tomorrow there will be less, the wreckage carted out
to landfills overflowing with conviction.
Tomorrow stretches out its arms, embraces the present
perfect continuous: Have. Have *been*. Emerging.
Tomorrow is the afterworld, a surface unbroken
by need: life forms engulfed in never enough, pawing space
to breathe. That acetylene-scorched hand
clawing through rubble and ruin to clutch a first lungful.

PLOSIVE & FRICATIVE
for Jeramy Dodds

I

Accidents exterminated the T. Rex
Gave us the seedless grape
Text for the map of the present
State borders of Eastern Europe
This scar on my knee
The ability to see negative space
And its associative leaps, bounds
Of successive missions into outer spheres
Stations and probes
Scattered like Dinky cars on the stairs
When Dad came down
With popcorn and soda
To just unwind, *goddammit*
After a long, tiring day ...

II

Our larynx dropped, oh
150,000 years ago
Neurons pinging with potential
Yet it took a clumsy hunter-gatherer
One hundred millennia later
Readying a slate of obsidian
Under shadow of a paleolithic sun
Took a successful first blow
Bulb of percussion flowering
On the core, took her
That one confidence-builder to foresee
A second strike flaking usefully

A being on the verge –
Thumbnail splitting
CO_2 impelled past teeth
The first fully formed expletive
Making itself heard

III

The wheel was pared down
In the imaginations of labourers
Pushing a plough through their fields
Trying on different sounds
Thinking out loud
This scene replayed circa 3500 BC
In three areas of the globe
Three protoscientists
Hitting on *round*
All at once

Sumerian and Chinese axles
Hitched to dumbfounded bovines
Scoring furrows, rounding corners
While the third avatar
Holed up in his workshop
Across the fat blue horizon
A father foremost, makes of the sun-shape
Toys for his rugrats
Toys unseen in the whole chiefdom
Kickshaws, gewgaws
To be hurrahed at

IV

Whether the boy heard the low, viscous hiss
Of pierced inflatable
Over the *thwack-thwack* of hockey card
Clothespinned to the frame
Rhyme's engine chugging
Past diamonds, monkey bars
The downslope freshly asphalted
Delivering the car-free rush
That comes with growing up unimpeded
Hands hovering
Above the handlebars, tempting
Speed demons

The wobbly front wheel
Snaking a determined path
Towards the gravel shoulder
The bicycle brought low
Forelegs before hind, skewered
By the ur-arrow

V

A chert blade
No bigger than a white lie
Dug up in Brighton, Ontario
And dated, as these things are
To a past cherished for
Unassumed lakes and skies
Uninterrupted corridors

Alit on my palm
Triangulating the trips and pratfalls
Of the species jerk
Its face scarred, flaked
Fluted from tip to base
To let the blood or fit the shaft

Gather close, listen
To the distant knapper
Evolving as we speak

Shh

The day after his wife left him,
Charles found a bucket of antimatter
in the basement. He was rummaging for
their wedding album, packed away
in the canvas suitcase, years back.
It was rainy, hydrogen atoms coalesced
on the windowpane; he wiped a tear
from his face, tossed aside two boxes
of summer clothes, a tickle trunk
of unused toys – and there it was,
storm-front grey, tagged with rust,
impassively betraying the laws
of physics. Charles put a lid on it
right away. This he understood.
A microgram would get him to Mars,
the rest beyond the heliopause
under the canopy of kinder stars.
He began pilfering necessities
from the lab. Pens and Post-its,
a frayed flight manual tucked
inside his jacket. Thursday he snuck
a magnetic nozzle thruster
past Phil at security. What on earth
would his wife think? He duct-taped
her picture to the garage wall,
worked into the wee hours. Oh,
how she used to draw him out,
the static that tore from her skin
to his, waking him into percipience.
He redoubled his efforts, fashioned
a fuel cell and feed system trussed
with broom handles. Just seconds

ahead of the launch, Charles hugged
the bucket to his chest and wept
a last time. So lucky
to have found it. Coldness
seeping through his rib cage towards
the simple matter of his heart.

PATENT #A102520

Head-Mounted Apparatus for Noetic Augmentation

Disclosed is a sheer foil of titanium – possibly
tungsten, any transition metal so long as it's silvery
and you can see your face. Subject's hat size is
a factor. Sheet tips are soldered together to form
an open-ended cylinder, one aperture designated
'the up side,' crowned by a dozen copper filaments
with electromotive adhesive. Yes, these will pick up
cosmic noise, at levels easily ignored. To address
wave plurality, a dial (black, preferably) affixes
to the back, in notched degrees, 10 amperes each.

See representative drawing, markers E and H.

Turned on, the antennas act as conduits for buzz –
resonant thought of a subset within time frames
finite, a.k.a. the zeitgeist. Metaphysics tells us
ideas are collusions of mind and matter. This device
separates one from the other, the better to boost
transference. Very user-friendly. Expect eurekas.

NB: Design modifications recommended
only if conceivable.

It is always all ways there,
where the halide floods square off the desert's pianissimo,
stand to their singular care: lighting the yard.
The hum? A refrigerator in the small hours.
Voltage marches through barbed wire,
holds back the sagebrush. No wind, and this no-wind,
like a noble gas, pushes at the outside from the in.
There's a point there's NO TRESPASSING BEYOND:
a rattle, metal on metal that on first hearing
contracts the heart muscle, signals flux,
misdirection. Tracks half-arrive and just stop.
It's been like this from the start.

Occupying the space past the checkpoint
where you'd expect a hangar or warehouse to be,
a hangar or warehouse, whitewashed, windows near the flat roof
winched open. The night watchman treads the floor,
his steps unstack like Russian dolls, moving close to far.
There are no doors, and the idea that traffic
is unaccounted for – that takes some getting used to.

What's inside is by estimates more spacious
than outer dimensions permit. Like fMRIS, satellite photos
show pale green walls, a glow that bays
the surrounding negative. Intel radiates, that is
known. Unknown? –

                        Not the subconscious per se,
overstuffed banker's boxes, rows and columns waffled by
the Maglite's circle. Not nostalgia, crated, to the rafters.
Not a card catalogue for the nameless, faces
behind bars of a cage, keys on rings, rings on arrays
in the security office. Not alternate lives

cuffed and dragged underground to Room 101.
Just *you* in a continuous loop, reels of analog tape
before the splice. You as lumen, you as x-ray.

Loss increases speculation, speculation
kicks the generator a pitch higher. The terrestrial night continues,
envelops whatever you can see. Fence, tire marks,
graffiti bleed. The rest, those saccadic bits
our rods and cones pass over, are alien ephemera, gaps
in the field ... *now ... now ... now ...*
Right now. TOP SECRET. Classified.

THE ASTRONAUT

Whale song, a sound on
Voyager's Golden Record
waiting to be decoded

somewhere, like her.
Fuselage-drift. Porthole
rolls in a solar current.

Oceans, oceans of it.

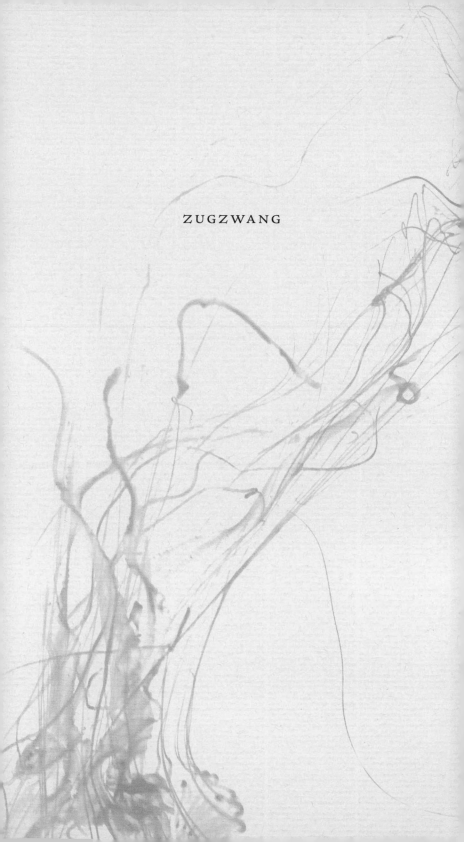

ZUGZWANG

KOINONIPHOBIA
fear of rooms

My life is a chain of thresholds
thrown up as a matter of course
by carpenters everywhere: jamb

and lintel aligned just so, door
swung wide ... walk-through
chock full of metaphor, the divide

between rational/not rational,
so easily crossed
by others. Once past it, I make

haste for the centre; calmer there
and better able
to take it in. The daybed

by the windowsill, chesterfield,
table lamps either side – all flaunt
with their impeccable taste

the compromised space of post
and beam, red brick defying
the 90-degree turns

of the chimney breast, cornice
and skirtings in collusion,
as if corners actually suspend

walls, their dervish run
on cardinal points, catapulting the
sense of without, within.

Just as I reach the concrete island, the don't-walk hand
don't flash. Spark plugs exhale, traffic switches,
drive-bys whip up a pedestrian typhoon. I could
jerry-rig a cot from light pole to light pole, wait it out
like Crusoe; prop a lean-to, pick the optimum bearing
for a signal fire. A semi gears up, screens the horizon,
crossing east to west, its panel painted with a
gargantuan Vachon 1/2 Moon. Vanilla.
Hunger pangs – they never lie. Castaway delirium
turns minutes into hours, days; I tally them
in blood on an inner cave wall, tiny Cheshire grins
that fan out, a swarm of treed cats, increasingly gap-toothed,
crazed. Years pass. Between sashimi ad nauseam
and dreams of the sea lane, I give rope to the claim
that time is not high tide autographing the beach
or thingness displaced in three dimensions,
but thought. Then I have one: maybe the South Pacific
is only a figment caused by a full bladder.
And this warthog's squeals and snorts? A UPS van
charging through the yellow. No matter. I think
that's him, coming to my rescue – my man Friday.
His iconic stride, his aura of operating-theatre white.

She spoke of the sides then, the angle made right,
one part thataway, another this, snapping a napkin
from its tin coffin and smoothing it straight
next to her latte. Uncorked a pen
and set to work, tongue between lips, each line
issued freehand, the Uniball's path
nibbling pores of the tissue, bleeding the design.
I'd just enough afternoon left, a curious air and half
a decaf *in situ*, plenty of reason to wait out excuses,
though yes, the a/c was on the fritz,
and I was uneasy, overheated – okay, truth is,
face to face with Celeste, after last week, beat me witless,
and the woozy mess she was making
of that polygon was a welcome distraction
from our listing history. She'd do the thinking
for both of us, abstraction

by subtraction. 'See here,' she said, aiming the nib
at the joint of legs *a* and *b*, 'ground zero.'
A biscotti crumb near the vertex turned squib
with a flick of her index. 'We know
we met. What's unclear is how
we parted inside. Nevertheless, you're over there
and both sides squared net us the here-and-now
of length *c*.' She always did have a flair
for the pragmatic. Hair ambushed at the crown
by matter-of-fact elastic, a staple hinge in her
glasses. Ache came the long way round,
pushed past happenstance to engineer
the denouement. 'QED,' she said,

'distance from yours to mine, the root of two.
Which is *irrational*, sunshine.' The words whistled
(on account of her chipped tooth) clean through

my neocortex. None of this made any sense
to begin with, her being Aquarius, me a Leo,
the trippy way we first knocked skulls, the entrance,
stage left, of the tubby cherub, that final peal
of consciousness. Had I not come to?
The past few months awash in a pinkish haze, today
resuming normal hues. It's the déjà vu
that makes the hurt more vicious. 'This latte,'
she summed up, tapping the glass, licking off
her sexy foam moustache, 'this latte was simplex
delicious. You dig?' Clearly, we were over. A cough
brought the waitress, separate cheques,
a late revelation: I saw Celeste
escape the demands of the present in sensible shoes
and a shapeless dress, head west-northwest
towards her future, the long march of the hypotenuse.

The sun a sprung

sprocket. Sky atilt:
new buds squeak
through. Moon's
a movable pulley,
alley cats mewling

like penitents. Sense
coils from ignorance,
effect begets cause;
outside our windows
the core falls ... fast

into Newton's laws.

He imagines *now* on the rack.

A slower-than-thou dolly zoom at the climax.

Neurotransmitters shooting the rapids.

¤

Imagines his right calf is a crystal container of indeterminate volume, filled up over a ten-count, emptied, filled again, each second spit out like a polynomial.

¤

The day-after an all-nighter in his thalamus.

There's a blob in his brain and consciousness is a klieg light that casts amorphous shadows on the body. He's sure of this: he's swallowed a jellyfish.

¤

He remembers the manikin strung up at the front of the high school lab, how squinting didn't make it any less ominous, less hominid.

Remembers he's in love. No one else has access, no one can say his love is illusory. There's no such thing as unfelt love.

¤

Hears a pen-click in the cerebrum.

Thinks, *inventory*.

The bare bulb hangs like every wrong-headed idea
    I've ever had. Glass blown smooth
    as guilt, filament fitful, the animal
behind the blink. Sulphur-whiff
and sweat-musk, chiaroscuro
    along the east wall, Chandleresque. For me, the hero,

they left a coffee, blood-thick. A crumpled cigarette,
    one match. Permission to be
    alone: a poor man's liberty.
The mind paws debris, overturns
stones, finger-traces patterns in
    mud. X's are me, the O's, him. Tit for tat begins.

We did it, sure. Pals since we were kids: 'Here comes
    trouble's twin,' they'd say, called me
    Turtles and it stuck, a tender piece
between molars; been working its
canker juice ever since. True
    names are for taxpayers, only players make do

with games. I know my Hamlet, the savage indecision
    damp air brings on, the subtle
    double vision of the one-way
reflection, a doppelgänger's darker cast.
Sell him out. I hear it soft, a soughing
    in the ear. Logic's a stock ticker, allowing

no emotional error, no conflicting report – my sentence
    will be lighter when I give it up.
    Five years, assuming he sings too,

but if he uncuffs fetters of self-interest
and swallows his words; if my abettor
       falls on his sword, I'm scot-free. Does fatuity make for a better

man? I can see him now, shirt sleeves rolled past biceps,
       crossed arms a marker, a shield
       from cops good, bad, the strategy
of opposites: epithets and empathy, truths
and escape routes laid out like testaments
       to Nietzsche, finding morality in ego, intelligence

in the rat. No need to imagine his situation as
       any different from mine. Rules
       are what define the trap:
symmetry, the State's last laugh.
This water tip-tapping a path through
       the elbow-maze of station pipes, he hears it too,

wets his lips, as I do, releases the same helium thought:
       we'd get 12 breezy months
       if we both kept mum. Not
the best outcome but close, altruism
endorsed, the ability of ethics
       to square the circle. It's one thing to know the facts,

another to deal with them. A con's thirst for preservation
       is his curse. My boy ain't Kant,
       he's a reprobate, same as me, no
co-operate in the vocab. Is there honour
in stupidity? Million-dollar question, natch.
       Coffee gone cold, I lip the cigarette. Strike the match.

A flipper slices the surface glare, a pinion.
Sin, young and fruitful in Gideon.
Little Boy, then Fat Man.

A staircase, a zipper.
Big Dipper and high-flying Orion.
Death-defying gladioli line the Colosseum.

ALASKAN BLACK COD
AT THE ST. LAWRENCE MARKET

No formula forbids time, t, from wending
backwards. Cod swim forward, that's all
they know. The fishmonger's blade unzips
its coat; two fillets flipped open, mid-book.
From a distance, d, the ribs look like lined sheets
awaiting words. Though *like* doesn't change
what's white and meat. Flesh is kinship, I'm told,
but my pretensions transcend polypeptides.
Luckily, the universe spins only one way:
clockwise. History gives me a leg up, a vision
of ancestral pools, slick and nitrous, hissing
through rock; some idea, too, about the makeup
of my food, a giant's tooth on the scale, mass, m,
under a kilogram. Dinner for two, the man's smile
a scratched lotto card. And the tale of the cod?
Calories. Hundreds lost to picture that prelimbed
creature at Ocean's brim. There's one timetable,
one through force, F, and I'll take my share as if
I had a choice. That'll have to do for the fish.

Homo sapiens sapiens
frighten easily. That's why
we're still around to throw up constructs
that *have* doors, understand concepts

like genetic drift, daydream. Alone
we are nothing if not fit
to answer the odd knock –

the price of clear and present
is cheapened thought, plastic casino chips
 in a cranial bucket. What wins out

comes naturally. Loping
across shag, sock on fibre sparking
bonfires in the tenth dimension. Yes,
the other D's, whorls beyond
 our load-bearing three.

 There
are creatures there
who see anthropoid shadows
as heavenly phenomena. How do we
receive them? It takes a speciation

 to perceive
the counterintuitive: particulate
has the ability to be
in multiple planes simul-

taneously. Any simian
can undo a latch. The smart ones
press an eye to the peephole, watch
back.

Sometimes it just clicks right off the start and sometimes you have to work at it. Luckily for us, it has just been clicking from the start. We keep working at it and it has been progressing.
— *Alexander Steen, Maple Leafs rookie*

The click is the ice-tap of stick
Morseing for the puck. It starts –
a drop pass to the King of Hearts,
the one who's been there, kicks
in twice for each pearl of sweat,
takes luck for all it's worth, tosses,
turns, pulls out a no-look crisscross
from the dregs of 110 percent,
bevelled blades jigging his signature
into the sheet. True work's a measure
of headway. Break it down: applied force,
distance travelled. Perseverance,
sonny, *that's* nature's crowning joule,
the huff, the puff, the give, the go-al.

THE CHESS PLAYER
for Geoff Tierney

Abstract

Theory:
the ideal position is the first,
each move a further weakness,
a giving way of perfection.
In this sense,
the game is meaningless.

Reykjavik, 1972

The needle in a haystack, Bobby Fischer,
America's crackerjack prize,
arrives with a Kissinger send-off
and a priest for a second
in ever-grateful Iceland.
Waiting there, the 'lazy Russian bear' –
Boris Spassky, regime's crafted mien,
learned, ear tuned
to opera, the urbane observation.
When you pull the large half of the wishbone,
what you forge: a sickle, a star.

Two generals,
one parapet.

On the TV
hangs a square, divided into 64,
two-dimensional pawns, knights,
kings and queens claiming
areas of dark light.

My Brother, the Prodigy

At seven, freckles like splotches
of rain on a window,
cheeks stubborn still
with baby fat, he'd sit, knees on the chair,
countenance of an overseer
in a school play.
The five-move combination, attacks
that left his pieces in disarray,
all-for-one free-for-all,
face expressionless
as an Oompa-Loompa.

Dad would say
I was a different-type player,
positional, difficult to beat, and truth is
though nearly as good
I was not nearly as spectacular
and at nine, destined to be
perpetually
two years older.

The Royal Game as Tool

Memory, spatial ability, fortitude.
Throughout history, rulers
take to the board against masters,
practice the act of sacrifice.
The good player is vatic,
reckoning lines of advance
with a twitch,
a drumroll in the temples.
Success easily marked with check, check,
mate.

Ah, the double entendre,
poor hapless Mirandas
played false by brave Ferdinands.
Chess lends love its rules,
bends a knee, pillows up subtext,
makes hard men humble
between despair and ecstasy.

So it is now, show and tell,
an adman's shorthand, the savvy consumer
duped by laughable scenarios
in pitches for tampons, car rentals,
financial counselling, stereos.
Between the rhetoric
a knight's wooden head curling
a bearded question mark.
What's Rorschach for smart?

Match of the Century

The Cold War made metaphor
a sport, victory by icon,
brain into brawn.

The men, specimens.
Fischer complained
of frequencies beyond our species' range.
The Soviets beachcombed the hall
for mind-controlling devices
hidden by the CIA.
One Red agent whiffed
an empty bag around the table
and sealed it, labelled
AIR FROM STAGE.

Game 6, Spassky swivels his chair
to mimic Fischer's side-to-side,
playing to the back row
like two dead men dancing.
In defeat, an overture – the lazy bear
joins the hall's applause.

Fischer's only match
the tussle with his psyche:
audience too near, TV cameras
too loud, poor illumination.
Late for every game.
The fear of winning.

Game 13,
Spassky left guillotined,
the matrix manifest before him.
An unwinnable position won
by the high school dropout,
the *nyekulturni*.

A new world champion.
Shades of Rasputin
on the cover of *Time*.

The Prodigy Grows Up

Dad once turned down
a Russian master who approached
with hopes of coaching
the inscrutable reedy-haired kid
and his big brother.
We got printed T-shirts instead:
mine, *I Pawnder All Knight*,
his, *I'm a Chessnut*.

When our ages went double-digit
we were versed in the merits
of well-rounded individuals.
We made time for friends, hockey,
piano lessons after school.
Chess was the monster
in the closet, ready to pounce.
We saw the kids it ate, they were
the ones we'd lose to.

Still, we'd study.
Weekends in our pyjamas,
Bobby Fischer Teaches Chess
at the dining room table.

Nationals, under 16:
my brother, as usual, winning –
but I was unbeatable, the draw king.
Until the game against
the second seed, when I silver-
plattered a bishop sacrifice
and won, thinking
so this is what it's like
to be my brother.
Then didn't win another.

The Shannon Number, 10^{120}

There are more games of chess
to be played than atoms
in the universe.

Each sit-down at a board,
an ad hoc teleport.

Deep Blue

It's no secret
the best among us
are bested by ones and zeros.
Curious, though, that we don't lose
repeatedly, matches a saw-off:
one for the mainframe, one for the suit.
A million ticks per second
sometimes
no equal for intuition,
that foggy blue nightlight.

The digitally fashioned victory
is no less a stroke of one
in the win column.
So say some.
Others discern
intelligence in the means,
never a measure of brute force
but a process: carbon-fused art.

Playing the Endgame

Fame became infamy.
Fischer disappeared
into catacombs of misery,
into the streets of California.
Cinched his paranoia, pulled tight
the zippers and snaps:
Soviet agents had poisoned his water, or
the world was to end
unless it didn't, and then
was to end again, more fester

and condemnation.
His obsession with body secretions,
Hughesian.

A half-Jew
who admired Hitler
for imposing his will.

1992, Yugoslavia, triumph put on ice
when he trumps Spassky
despite years away
from top-flight competition
and the unmet demand for
his hotel toilet seat
to rise higher than everyone else's.

Zugzwang

My brother turned out.
It's the moves we don't make
that make us.

That's me,
my back to the room
in the alternate universe,
pondering the two young men
hunched like parentheses,
the game between them.

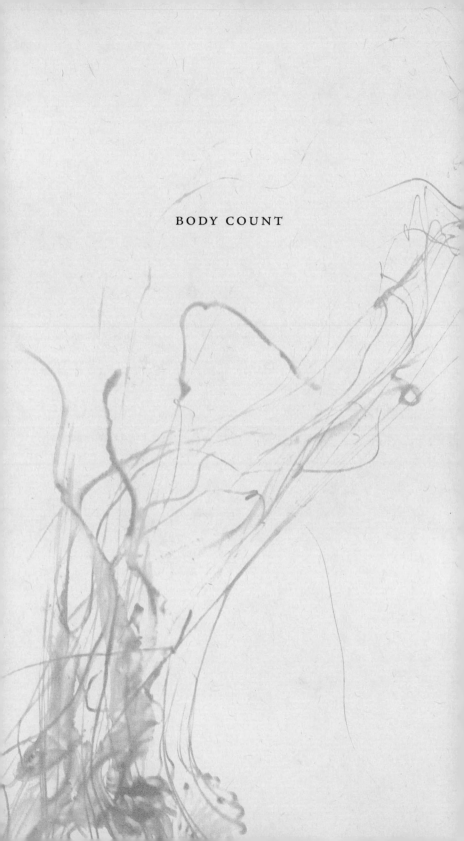

BODY COUNT

Stick a corpse, a well-meaning prod
and watch the worm slip its throat –
an ass for a head, head for an ass –
alas, an inauspicious place to start.
To know one from the other is less
battle than war, a lifelong skirmish
between the Admiral and the whores.
Still, we've come this far, and fairly.
Generations of tried-and-true mutations
tripping towards that fare-thee-well.
Screw art; praise the orbitofrontal
for a change, the diffuse nebula of
risks and rewards operating fist-size
above the eyes. Ballast for a full life:
you do this, you get that, you genius
you. Think Yorick and his gibes, not
the imbecile with the skull puppet
waxing melancholic six feet above
the orchestra pit. Jab *him*, stick *him* –
the ratio of poke to grin is around
one to one. Laugh, groundling, laugh.

CHRONOMENTROPHOBIA
fear of clocks

The unblinkered face glints, beguiles
pale rays of the sputtering wick –
movement beneath it apace

with moon over sky, tricking one
into a belief of set
and rise. Logic demands symmetry,

the periodic, no-nonsense click
harnessed to a glassy sheen
while gear trains ration out lives

in intervals of less.
Listen closely: pendulums
heavy with night. The weights fall

like a last, long-drawn breath
sealed in a mahogany casket.
Intricacy comes to this:

time trapped by mechanics,
the piezoelectric tic
of quartz, caesium-133 switching

tracks. Ever tighter stitches.
Everywhere hours dispatch seconds.
Cellphones, towers, pixelated

billboards, wrists.

Seven, eight, nine,
another by the ceiling, Lefty with the lame wing
rowing circles on the sill. Blue-collar boys. Yellowjackets
dive-bombing the chloramine sheen

of the greasy grill's
freshly cleaned front window. Five o'clock shadow,
three-alarm BO: that's me forking cold hash round my plate,
looking for a corner. Self-conscious

and consciousness of self –
double bummer. I hold up the palm of my spoon
like a rear-view mirror: a world gone concave. Snap-to
the patter of exoskeletons bouncing off

transparence, a sound
apt for impending violence. The Sports,
rolled swiftly, a billy of statistics, of successes of men,
ushers Lefty's end. Immediate

regret, followed by waves
of empathy. I leave the others to their paths,
a squadron flighting as metaphor, dumbing it down
for the breakfast crowd still bleary

from the night that was.
Mere feet to the right, the front door, propped
open, provides irony a means of escape; customers pass
freely, braincases unbruised

and sapience intact
in any literal sense, going about their breathing,
busily believing a founder or foundress will take them
straight through the corporeal

glass ceiling. I set aside
the newspaper, do my best to will the wasps
towards the entranceway. As useless gestures go, at least
hopeful. The numinous buggers continue

jonesing for the sky on
the other side. Stupid, stupid insects. I watch them
earn their haloes for a while. Smile, and sigh. And then
ritually clean the butter knife on my thigh.

What strikes when the dump truck trundles by
    isn't its guttural bass
or how shadows dog it under the syrupy April sun,
    but pigeons; in unison
two dozen of them take to air, one dark ungainly
    creature whose brain
fires again and again with fear and its resolution;
    like an orchestra that picks up
the principal theme with a flick of the conductor's
    wand and yet alters it
with context, the same before-and-after that grips
    us all, shipshape
in this pocket of time: me, the truck driver, the old
    woman shawled against
the mild wind, passersby following the parkette's
    curve, heading off towards
other movements as the pigeons diagram an arc
    from matte black earth
to uplifted branches of the still-bare birch; then
    sway there restfully,
a uniformed string section certain of its phrasing.

Emily has dropped to second place in the list of popular baby names. She came into the internet café to google herself. Time she has plenty of, it's pooling inside her; plus the guy one screen over is cute. He looks familiar. She wonders what number he comes in at, whether he's winning or losing the other race. When he leaves, she follows at a safe distance, checks both ways before crossing. Three blocks later, she falls in love with the drape of white T-shirt over his shoulders. She imagines a lifetime of this, gumshoeing around corners, chasing down a name, a face to match. At the streetlight, the guy flips a coin into a busker's case, lights a cigarette. Emily crouches on one knee, goes through the motions of untying and retying. She remembers junior high, her first real crush. What would seven years have done to him? What will the next seven do to her? If only the course of true love were beyond proof; at some point in the story, every private eye has to present her case. The guy starts forward, pauses beside the black gates of Philosopher's Walk, and Emily picks up her pace. Too late. He turns and steps into nothingness. Reaching the archway, she's lost him among the milling students. *Oh, number two* – 'Michael!' she yells. Every boy in the vicinity rotates his head.

Shot through with gut rot, perched on the edge
of Revelations. The guppies, Judd and Nelson,
dead in their tank, *M*A*S*H* muted on the tube,
kettle turning it loose, footloose, *oowhee, Marie* –

The voice in your head's got a bad case of uptalk.
Fire the ciggie off the burner, Grandma's trick
when they took away her matchbooks. Torque
tight the D cells in the flashlight, head outdoors.

Forage for Cheetos at corner after corner store,
settle on a Sesame Snap. A dead ringer for
Darryl Sittler's asleep in the back of a soft-top
Eldorado. Whatever became of the pillars? Bono,

Geldof, you know, righting the wrongs, four
on the floor. If only you'd been punk enough,
in the day, maybe goth. Pink shirts with collars,
who'da thought? Run a shopping cart through

the Hudson's Bay display, bask in the alarm
until the cops show in retro yellow cruisers.
Beat it, they say, as if it wasn't really your fault,
your pain. As if. Shards cover the pavement

like asteroids. You'd cough up all the quarters
between the cushions for one hit of hyperspace,
a chance to set aflame all that mega-hold mousse.
Somewhere off in the inner ear, a Molotov

cocktail hitting its mark, the slap of deck shoes
down Yonge. Echo of the bust, generation of
the day after. Never more than six degrees from
what's-his-face to you: *reductio ad absurdum*, boyo.

and throwing off the covers, stepping over islands
of dirty laundry to face the bathroom mirror.
Those purple slippers under my eyes. Imagine
a needle pushed into my forehead, clear through
overlapping probabilities
of skin, skull, grey matter
to emerge on the other side, stuck
into the drywall. Yet I'm stubborn. Bristles
against gums. Shower, and water runs over my neck.

Stock footage for the existential set: tub slip, careless
bus driver. The subway ferries
thought experiments, devices systolic,
now diastolic. To glimpse a subatomic being,
feel sorry for it. Express with jaw fixed
or slack, relaxation of the procerus, pupil dilation.

Platform light contracts behind us.
Within, a tunnel-muffled cough.

It's a spar with cotton batting.

It's a fuck-you to non sequiturs in polite hallucinations.

It's what-have-you-done-for-me-lately, ringmaster Bately.

It's Shark Week on the Discovery Channel.

It's lunch: white tuna on toast, two Kraft Singles, a coffee, black.

It's the little boy inside, struggling with asthma, insomnia, self-
esteem, freefall, certainty, smack.

It's like believing you're destined for great things, only the reverse.

It's loaded dice dangling from a rear-view, a siren's surround
sound, a car crash on mute.

It's the waiting, it's perverse.

It's four walls, the couch and the remote, a carpet like the Sahara.

It's the facts, bulleted, PowerPointed, *poof*.

It's like nothing you imagined, it's better than what's worse.

It's psychosomatic, can't you see, think happy thoughts.

It's three clicks at most.

It's time for a haircut.

It's God being God, numbering the atoms in our universe,
losing count, starting over, moving on to the next.

It's ten to the power of whatever.

Is it hell? Maybe yes.

It's sticky, like Gobstoppers stolen from Mac's Milk.

It's that baby tomahawk the doc swings to test your tendon reflex.

It's there in the confessional, the made-up, piddling sins
guaranteeing a breezy penance.

It's me, it's all me, and I'm stuck with him, aiming his pecker
when we piss, jamming fingers down each other's throat
to see who vomits first.

It's the *idea* of the paper cut.

It's what's worse.

It's what's worse.

It's what's worse.

Slipped into with a breaststroke, twill tape tied at the nape,
if nimble enough, around your waist. The rear gap, a fig leaf,
lets in an emollient breeze. Hospital gowns, the colour of
semi-private, of night's seams. Hours wound like copper

between rounds, Tylenol 3s, Gravol to keep it down. One
bed over, the fellow is always young, in the scheme of things
a pipsqueak, certain of discharge. Him also, ministered to
by the able-bodied, unimpressed until the end – he'll crawl

into it. Everywhere that sea-serpent green, thread counts
wearing thin, so many washings in bleach. This won't be
the gown I expire in, a few cycles still: release and admittance,
release, admittance. The ability to adapt, unremitting, given

knowledge of the limit, 52 cell renewals, no more, probably
less. Cursed, blessed, or hung up in between? As an either-or,
better than nothing, I guess. Each next contains the last, like
my new bunkmate; he snores, in the wake his encased femur

knitting. Tomorrow, I'm for home. Civilian clothes. Cotton
and synthetics, blended to hold shape. Thermal underwear,
wool sweater, heating layers within, nuclei making a go of it,
ghosting another version I labour to flourish, and forget.

AULOPHOBIA
fear of flutes

Bruegel's soundtrack.
Each note bereft, prescient. Death
needs you to listen, leads

like the Pied Piper, phalanges clicking
open-hole keys. His chosen
instrument, light

as the breath over your shoulder,
a loved one about to speak.
That's the crux,

isn't it? Lucidity often fools us.
We follow symbolism at our own risk
in the hippocampus,

down rabbit holes, unearthing
dark incidents. An age before
fife and drum, an angel blew a kiss

across a sharp-edged mouthpiece,
a lumbering soul knocked
two holes in a mammoth bone, and Pan

cut down the reeds for his pipes.
That first melody, so clear, a lament
for Syrinx, imagining

he held her in his hands.

Briefly, now, I drive between them,
harvesting countrysides between charmed
and foolproof moorings.
                                    – Don Coles

Passing is nearly all approach, the steady, *steady now*
of holding course as the landscape morphs gently
into a larger version of itself. The specks become
trees, become roadside rest stops,
become what they always were
when they were distant and irresolvable.
Constant motion counterfeits stillness,
and if not for the eye's reassurance
we'd have no sense of progress, though progress,
in turn, demands its own measure,
some thought for the to and the from.
Briefly, now, I drive between them,

more or less the point where
my birth's as near as the other is far,
these 30 or 40 years held in place for
an unfurling of highway in perfect pitch.
Give consolation its due: things could have
gotten worse when bad – or good –
and they didn't. Or if they did,
they did so so smoothly it wasn't worth
noticing. Many times I've taken this route,
shuffling short-lived asides on the long term,
harvesting countrysides between charmed

and not-so-charmed towns, their population counts
growing small in the side mirror. Each drive
happens only the once, though it seems otherwise
when the images pile up, the farmhouses,
the Shield rock, ploughed fields and For Sale signs,
odometer cresting, my hands on the wheel
at an easy five and ten o'clock.
A candidate for my older self settles
with the hum, takes its semblance
from the windows' reflections, and he simply *is*,
for a time, as I am, among unassuming
and foolproof moorings.

Evenings, I crisscross King Street
and avoid the panhandlers, spare a glance
to see whether I'm being

tailed. My route, plotted on the xy-plane,
tracks supply and demand
to its conclusion. Home

and tired, throwing out flyers, charitable appeals,
free gym memberships. Impulse is
formulaic. Over time

I will take my place in line
alongside the velvet rope. This is who I am:
perforated packaging, disposable contacts,

a healthy platelet count. Sum
equal to the parts. Off the subway at 6:07 p.m.,
every heartbeat disperses

2.4 ounces of blood, retina
converting wavelengths of the visible
into electrical pulses, I weave

my way towards the exit. A stray hand
sifts coins in my pocket, capillaries flow
with the necessary oxygen

to carry on. Topside, empty coffee cups
in fists, like white-lipped howls.
The lightless figures behind them.

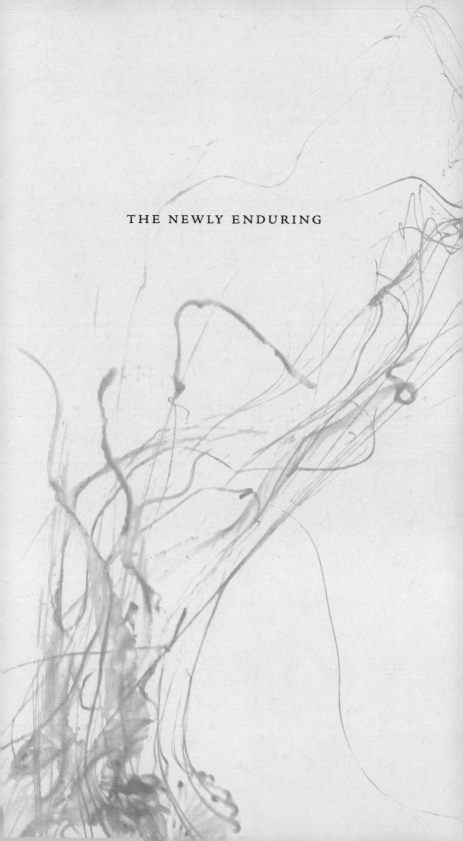

THE NEWLY ENDURING

AUTOBIOGRAPHY

Being is miscible. Into the vast pool

a scruple of present, our inner alchemist

calibrating elements at hand until

a transmuted thought fogs the beaker.

Memory. Base notes of a perfume fill

the just-emptied elevator, a voice falls

out of range – the dial stops, collapses

to one frequency, a deciphered emotion

that trips the wire. The surprise is, we're

surprised: an instant in our story long

since forgotten, irreducible sediment

of processes quick and silver. Meanwhile,

cast back from the everyday burble,

these watery selves, bright with reflection.

Ray woke into adulthood and tore down all
his WWF posters. Squashed The Rock into a snowball,
rolled him under the bed. Swept
Gameboy cartridges off his desk, lidded last night's
leftover airplane glue. Before the mirror,
he watched flecks of chest hair sprout, curl;
his Adam's apple dipped so fast,
reflection worked on a half-
second delay. He was going places, image already
making good time, pecs defining his sternum
as the white line down a northern
Ontario road. Today he warranted
another coat of underarm deodorant.
Extra heft reverberated on each stair, straight
towards the kitchen for some All-Bran,
coffee. Jowls coming in nicely, neck
squatting like a weightlifter into the collar
of the new button-up, Father's gold watch
inherited with one sharp motion
around his wrist. A briefcase appeared in the den.
Life was loosening its middle; memories popped
into pneumatic tubes: TURNING POINTS, ANECDOTES,
REGRETS, etc., hither and thither before the *shink*
of keys to the convertible sent
a flush right to his prostate.

Ray opens the door on a 24-karat sun.
The lawn, gleaming. A two-door garage
eyes him from across the street. He picks the paper
up off the mat, folds headlines
into a hand heavy with a platinum band.
Back molar hurts – years since

he's seen a dentist. Trick knee, carpal tunnel,
nothing new that can't be soothed,
massage and sauna, ad infinitum. Smiles
crack on the driveway; Ray marches into the glare,
match-perfect, unaware of the tiny nose
pressed against the second-floor window,
the DNA samples left on the glass.

Astronomy Night, Grade 4, mittens wet from snowballs
chucked at snot-nosed Marcus, we squint through
pinhole telescopes, sawed-off Adidas shoeboxes, swear
on a shooting star. 'Meteor,' Mr. Felding corrects,
brown mohair jacket aglow, tobacco stains on bristles
of his moustache. Parents gaze down while we smartly
point out Venus. All of us, scientists, someday. Back then,
new discoveries were apples in the orchard. Remember
that note intercepted at morning recess? Reading it over
with Angela in the cloakroom? *That's* a name for a celestial
being. November 2003, she was where we were, on Earth,
consuming her share of microwaveables. Marcus too,
good sport, 40 percent chance he's losing his hair. Our
weekly inspection reveals greyer temples, a thinning hope
pinned to heavenly bodies. 2003 VB_{12}, where have you been
all our lives? They say Oort cloud, Caltech and Yale:
smaller than Pluto, colder than Mr. Felding's chalkboard
(cancer, 1999). Red for no discernible reason. Thirty-odd
years ago, did our clammy fingers pick you out of the lineup?
Seems possible. A mitten packs a whole lot of aim. But
we've learned finding brightness is easy – realizing you have,
as rare as a planet. Sedna, sweetie, you're a minor. They say
standing on your surface, a pinhead at arm's length would
eclipse the sun. Of course, all kids know heads of pins are
for dancing on.

XX

for C.

Dog-day cicadas up the drama, drumming
abdomen amphitheatres, squirrels chase their ideals
while a monarch knits, purls, remembers a mountain fir
in Mexico. This could be anytime, children amok
in the grass, lollipop smear over lip smacks,
collar jingle of the yellow Lab punch-drunk from
its olfactories. Each blade a finger pushed from
below, my own prints push back into earth … it was
dusk 1979 when I first kissed a girl, a girl named –
no. Is that really you beside me? We watch
top-heavy offspring, years away from independence,
clumsy as primal wishbone, downstroke, flight
of the archaeopteryx. Niche fillers. How many
of our many words come close to this willow's
photo-symphonic swell towards sun?
A blissful tot runs from her parents, two X
chromosomes, two legs the legs of the letter X
that could be you, my love, if the years were reversed
or re-versed, if history had no means to keep us
in place, in parallel, bound by this green space:
two adults, shelled. A honey bee backtracks
stigma to stigma, sterile, able through sister genes
to exist as though queen. The mindstruck hive,
and I hear in the fade of sustained chord
the tender you we have tried, tried
and failed. It's stunning anything's alive.

GELIOPHOBIA
  fear of laughter

You-know-who
always steals the show, ham-fisted,
doing his best Vincent

Price. Hobbes had it figured:
'expression of superiority' marched out
in mousy vowels –

neural paths drained like locks,
lungs (inexplicably)
hole-punched mufflers

dragged around the block. Canned,
contagious, harmonically pure
sign of psychosis, no wonder

there's a bandwidth of grey
between tickle and torture.
Dismiss the Rule of Three, the well-

placed banana peel,
priests and rabbis playing golf
with God. Its true appetite

is carnal. Abel's skull
staved in; Cain, rock in hand
and back arched, whoop

flung at the sky, the sky
swirling black.

Tuxedo scruff, Bozonian nose, eyes two hardboiled eggs,
whiskers of a lumberjack bivouacked in the bush for days –
undone by the double take, the thought-I-saw, the did!

and episodic justice dished to the Saturday-morning kids
who preside two feet from the glass, spoon Alpha-Bits
into champing mouths, milk drops raining chin to PJs.

Pshawing on the downbeat, 'Granny schmanny!' he says,
before the broom beats the brave out; he zags to its zig,
into the next cut. Back at it, the drafting table, letters fit

and fat for new readers: ROCKET LAUNCHER. The wick lit,
percussionist cued up, orchestra primed for succotash filet
when flame turns to flambé, when the shedding can begin.

Where big eats small, bigger eats big; Hector the bulldog,
grey as a chain link, guardian angel of the hydrocephalic
infernal whistling bird, snaps up pussycat in bear-trap jaws

until pounded out, ketchup style, by Granny. Applause
rounds out the natural order when the pussycat is flogged
and out pops canary. Bad is bad, and we are all full of it.

To catch one little bird, Sylvester gives free reign to the get,
firing its up-and-go like blanks to the brain, flow triggered
by a deep, sufferin' want that plucks the gut, sharpens claws,

bursts sibilants into slop. Who hasn't split a lip on the laws
of science? That there *felis silvestris* our furriest, furious regret
at being beholden to the stick of dynamite – fallible, fugged.

One bird leads to two, then three, repugnance and the (*gulp*)
end of the road. The hug of victimhood only 12 steps away:
'Fellow members, from now on my motto is, birds is strict-

ly for the birds.' Ah, willpower, desire is cliché, the id's
a-revvin'. Sylvester sucks Tweety's head – stuck! – halfway
through a straw, and we're okay with the shit-and-giggle,

his tantrums on linoleum. After all, he *is* a pussycat, kids,
undone by the double take, the thought-I-saw, the did.

Maximilian is mad for the end of the world. In his spare time, he writes fake obituaries for people he has loved. Wednesday, it's his Grade 3 teacher, Mrs. Weemer, whose overturned-bowl-shaped eyes made his throat hurt. Max takes care, works in an allusion to Florence Nightingale because she was the day's Final Jeopardy! question. The winning contestant wrote *what* instead of *who*, and Max hissed at the TV. Stupid paralegals – no survival skills. When nuclear winter arrives on *their* doorstep, they'll be fuelling up the snowblower. Fire, ice, it's all the same to him, as long as he gets a grenade launcher. He finishes up the obit just before his shift: 'Life bullies only those with tender souls.' Coming home from work early in the a.m., he pauses beside a guy asleep on the subway grate. Max, still wearing his Kinko's name tag, pretends to drop change in the coffee cup, kicks it over instead. Crosses the street quick as he can, coins rolling and rolling inside his head. Then he remembers Mrs. Weemer, scrubbing at his little scraped palms, trying to keep up with his sobs, and holds on tight. The spilt milk of her eyes. She's a dead woman, he thinks.

*What I'm doing is, if it is my time, I'd be cheating myself if I
did put more pressure on myself. I don't want to go out and say,
'This is my time and I don't want to go out and screw it up.'
Because if I do that, I'm screwing it up.*
> – Robert Esche, Flyers goaltender

There can be a long time between shots
in any game. Daydreams are photo ops

for the thinking man. First, water, a drink.
Settle on the parameters of your rink.

You're surrounded by thousands, idle
hands at their side, faces far and wide.

Choose a dozen people, assign personas,
histories, proclivities, as many etceteras

as you want. Factoids mimic the physical
properties of the vulcanized: black, fickle

and absorbing. Focus your powers on those
12 characters. Nobel laureates? War heroes?

Soup kitchen volunteers? Here's the rub:
one of them, at this moment, is screwing ub.

You've a job to do, Dr. Filby,
I understand. As you can see,
our filing is a bit behind. Ah, here it is,
a smoother case I've yet to witness,
no mean feat considering recent
loss of manpower to the flu.
Patient x-062 was quite senescent,
riddled with stomach cancer,
so our advice to her niece was
cephalic isolation, yessir, 'off
with the queen's head!'
Apologies, but take my meaning:
there is no longer a body
for you to autopsy. Trust me,
we made doubly sure she was dead
before beginning protocols,
the Institute cannot afford
to go through *that* again.

Let's be clear: transport personnel
are required to pass a rigorous
two-week class, review all manuals
prior to pronouncement. Now,
x-o-six-two was intubated
ahead of time, tub readied with ice,
replenished every hour. Never seen
such a slow agonal course, 72 hours
before she gave up the ghost.
Straight from deathbed to bath, cooling
helmet affixed, cardiopump working
like a Mexican without a visa.
O_2 Sat levels were high, 80 percent,

the bottom line there, page nine.
In this state – *intestate?* God help us!
Hah, just a little industry humour –
she was transferred to facilities here.
Prepped her myself in our new
state-of-the-art operating room.
Jugular sucking back a drip bag
of protectant, burr holes one-two
with the perforator. At this stage
the 'neuro' is removed.
Standard procedure, media circus
be damned. Surely, as men of science,
we agree: it makes perfect sense
to preserve only the brain.
Someday, Filby, someday
it'll be easily executed on any
general purpose nanosembler.
Like water over a riverbed, neurons
sliding this way, that, pooling
into a *you* or *me*. The body
simply a token, no more,
of the *esprit* immortal.

Forgive me, I get carried away.
Her head is vitrified over
in Bay 4. Care for a tour?

Honeycomb bones and soft tissue eddy about
the be that I yam, pop-eyed for the columns
of figures that run down four limbs, add up,
the dark matterstuff of my head, gunk from
the fingernail crescent from the barrel bottom.
Whiskey? Mind if I do. A body needs spirit.
Even sitting I'm moving, the well-worn hula
hoop around the sun, the microscopic jangle
of somatic cells. Yesterday left a caloric shiver
resonating among thermal fields and it cost me
me. Rust on the chassis, wind tugging follicles;
the legs of my single-malt sigh back to level.
Winter swirls these years like broth and I'm
no further no farther no father. It hurts to laugh.

LUTRAPHOBIA
fear of otters

It was grandfather who lost
his little toe. Waterdogs,
river weasels, a whole slick

pack of them, nipped the digit
while he was afloat in
the local watering hole. The old

country, this was, moonlit. *Kersplash*
he heard or thought so, turned
his head to see

three sinuous shadows
merge with the deep. Whiskers
brushed his thigh, rudders quick

past his flank. Perhaps
a game that went too far.
Though Granddad swore

one poked its kittenish skull
above the surface and froze him
with a warlock's eye. Ripples spread

to the banks. They would undulate
for years. 'That's silly,'
my son says, but I hold him tight

as a black-webbed claw
pushes off the tank's Plexiglas
inches from his ghost-green face.

Roaches laid open by minutens, arranged
in a glass box under rule of thumb, heirs

to irony without the wit to appreciate it.
Every indication is solidly in place.

Constants of the universe stack the deck
for carbon-based dominance – if only

we could reckon why the numbers are.
Pad Planck's minuscule h-bar and we're

adrift through living room walls, for example,
suddenly. Inspired fenestration, that's what

every home planet needs. Wainscotting, snake
plants, a phalanx of Marthas to descry

the feng shui no-nos. Beethoven's Fifth loud
in the background, making us all Romantics.

Yet however far we train the scope, a corner
ripples with Neil's flag. Reason evolved

to shoot for the moon, no? Hawking entered
God's mind while confined to a chair …

there, as good as any. Soak the dishes in
the sink, part the panel curtains. The night

above our kitchen is newly bright. Count
the stars. The final answer is everything, but.

ACKNOWLEDGMENTS

The opening epigraph is from 'Eclogue IV: Winter' by Joseph Brodsky, *To Urania* (The Noonday Press, 1992). The epigraph for 'Temperance St.' is from 'The Toome Road' by Seamus Heaney, *New Selected Poems, 1966–1987* (Faber and Faber, 1990). The quote for 'Sound Bite' is from the *Toronto Star*, October 3, 2005. 'The Chess Player' paraphrases a line from the song 'One Night in Bangkok,' lyrics by Tim Rice. 'The Day the Sky Turned Pink' dabbles in the song 'Footloose,' lyrics by Kenny Loggins. 'Puddy Tat' quotes the Warner Bros. short 'Birds Anonymous.' The quote for 'Sound Bite Do-Over' is from tsn.ca, March 18, 2004. The epigraph for 'These 30 or 40 Years' is from 'Driving at an Easy Sixty' by Don Coles, *How We All Swiftly* (Signal Editions, 2005).

Some poems first appeared in the following journals, magazines and anthologies: *Arc*, *Event*, *Eye Weekly*, *The Fiddlehead*, *IV Lounge Nights*, *Jacket*, *Maisonneuve*, *The Malahat Review*, *Prairie Fire*, *Strong Words: Year 2*, *This Magazine* and Torontoist.com. A special thanks to the editors of *Arc* for their continued support. And a shout out to littlefishcartpress for publishing *Seven Phobias*, a 'chipbook' of the phobia poems.

The Canada Council and the Ontario Arts Council provided much-appreciated financial assistance.

Several talented poets lent me their ears and helped shape the poems: Adrienne Barrett Hofman, Adam Dickinson, Jeramy Dodds, Ken Howe, Steve McOrmond, David Seymour and Andy Weaver. Thanks to Don Coles for kindly allowing me to borrow his lines.

Kevin Connolly is a flat-out great editor for his uncanny ability to ask the right questions and his calm bedside manner. Alana Wilcox, Evan Munday and Christina Palassio made me feel at home at Coach House, and are a pleasure.

Dear Charmaine, first reader, you walk the line between honesty and praise with grace. Thank you.

Matthew Tierney is the author of one previous book of poetry, *Full Speed through the Morning Dark*. He is a recipient of a K. M. Hunter Award for Literature, and won first and second place in *This Magazine*'s 2005 Great Canadian Literary Hunt. In the second year of his undergraduate degree, he switched majors from physics to English. He lives in Toronto.

Typeset in Adobe Jenson
Printed and bound at the Coach House on bpNichol Lane, 2009

Edited for the press by Kevin Connolly
Designed by Alana Wilcox
Cover photo, *Untitled*, April 2008, by Matt O'Sullivan
(www.thenarrative.net)
Author photo by Charmaine Tierney

Coach House Books
401 Huron Street on bpNichol Lane
Toronto ON M5S 2G5

416 979 2217
800 367 6360

mail@chbooks.com
www.chbooks.com